# T-Shirt art

by the editors of Klutz

KLUTZ

You have in your hands everything you need to make one-of-a-kind iron-on fabric transfers.

Use these patterns and idea-starters your own way by choosing colors, combining designs and adding special touches to create a unique look.

Get adult help to iron the transfers onto your clothes, and you'll end up with your own fab fashions.

# Here's what you get!

## plastic overlay

Slip it over a page before squeezing on the paint. You can use the overlay again and again. Zipper-style plastic bags or plastic page protectors will do in a pinch.

## ironing papers

This re-usable sheet (found inside the plastic overlay) protects your transfers during ironing. Parchment paper from the baking section at your grocery store will substitute nicely.

## Transfer paint

Six brilliant colors to use in your own brilliant way. Carefully cut the plastic case of paint off the book to start designing.

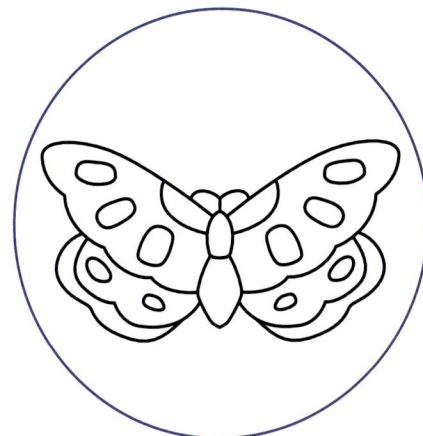

## Design Templates

Choose from more than 200 cool designs. Or create your own art.

# 101 T-Shirt Art

## 1 Choose a design.

## 2 Slide the plastic overlay over the page with your design.

*Cut the overlay out of the book with scissors, setting aside the ironing paper.*

**!** Stain Alert! T-shirt art is a fabric paint, and could make stains on your clothing, upholstery and rugs. So wear painting clothes, protect work surfaces, and work in a kitchen or outside.

4

**3** Squeeze your design onto the overlay.

*Give each bottle a good shake before using.*

*Work with one color at a time, letting each dry for about 30 minutes before adding the next.*

*If your design has an outline, paint that first and let it dry for 30 minutes before filling in with color.*

## How much paint?

TOO THICK
Won't bond to fabric

TOO THIN
Hard to peel up

JUST RIGHT

**4** Once your design is completely covered with paint,

wait...............
..........wait......
wait...for 24 whole hours until it's dry.

**5** Peel the transfer off the overlay, being careful not to tear it.

*Don't let the shiny side fold back on itself — if it does, gently pull the two areas apart right away.*

**6** Preheat a dry iron on the cotton setting.

*Cotton No Steam*

*Try out the iron on a test piece of fabric to make sure the temperature won't hurt it.*

**!** Always, always, always use the ironing paper when ironing down your design. If you don't, your transfer will stick to the iron, not your clothing.

**7** On an ironing board, put the transfer in place on your T-shirt.

*Lay it shiny side down and cover it completely with the ironing paper.*

**!** Get adult help when using a hot iron.

**8** Iron slowly back and forth over the transfer for 20 seconds.

**9** Press the iron along the edges of the transfer with the paper still in place.

**10** Let the transfer cool, then remove the ironing paper.

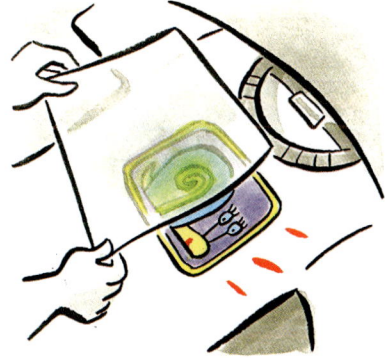

**11** Check that the edges of the transfer are well attached.

*If not, replace the paper and iron the edges again.*

# Laundry tips

Wash cold or warm

Line dry or dry on low

Turn clothing inside-out for washing

If the edges peel after washing, iron the transfer again with the ironing paper to set

7

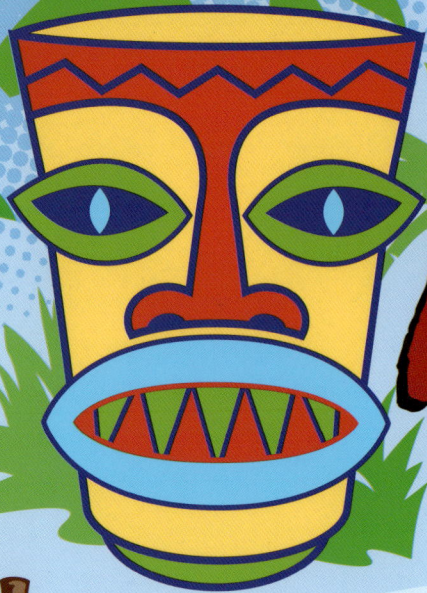

Island MADNESS

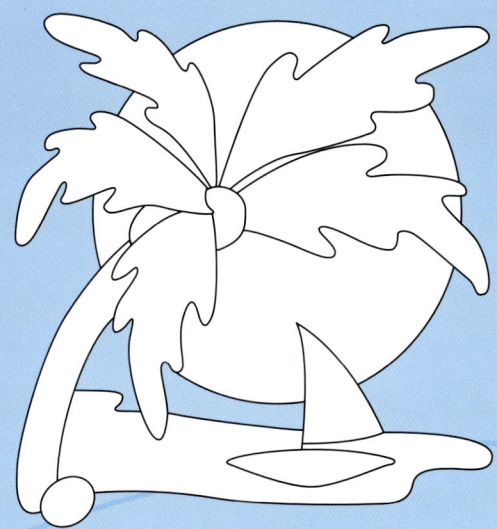

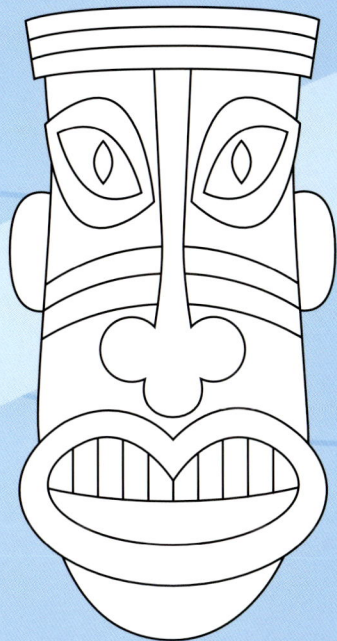

Surfer

Surfer

12

# Super Stars

We **KNOW** you're a star, now go show
the world with a Super-Star Tee!

aries

pisces

virgo

aquarius

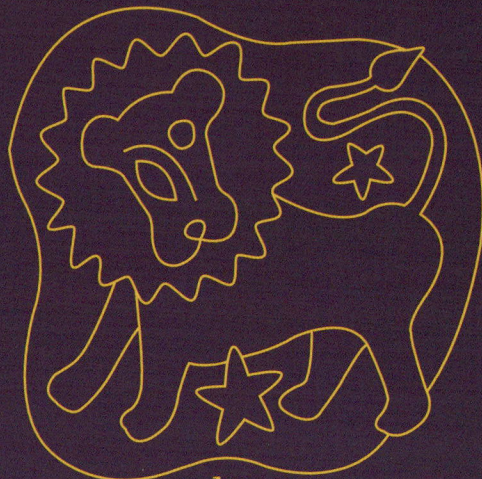

leo

*taurus*

*gemini*

*cancer*

*libra*

*scorpio*

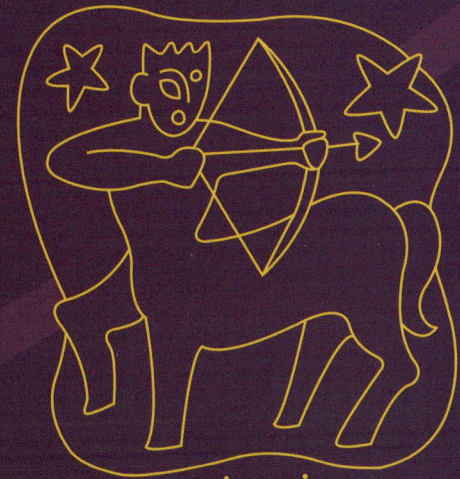

*sagittarius*

*capricorn*

*What's Your Sign?*

# Petals and Wings

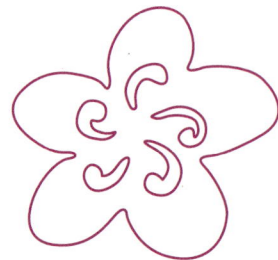

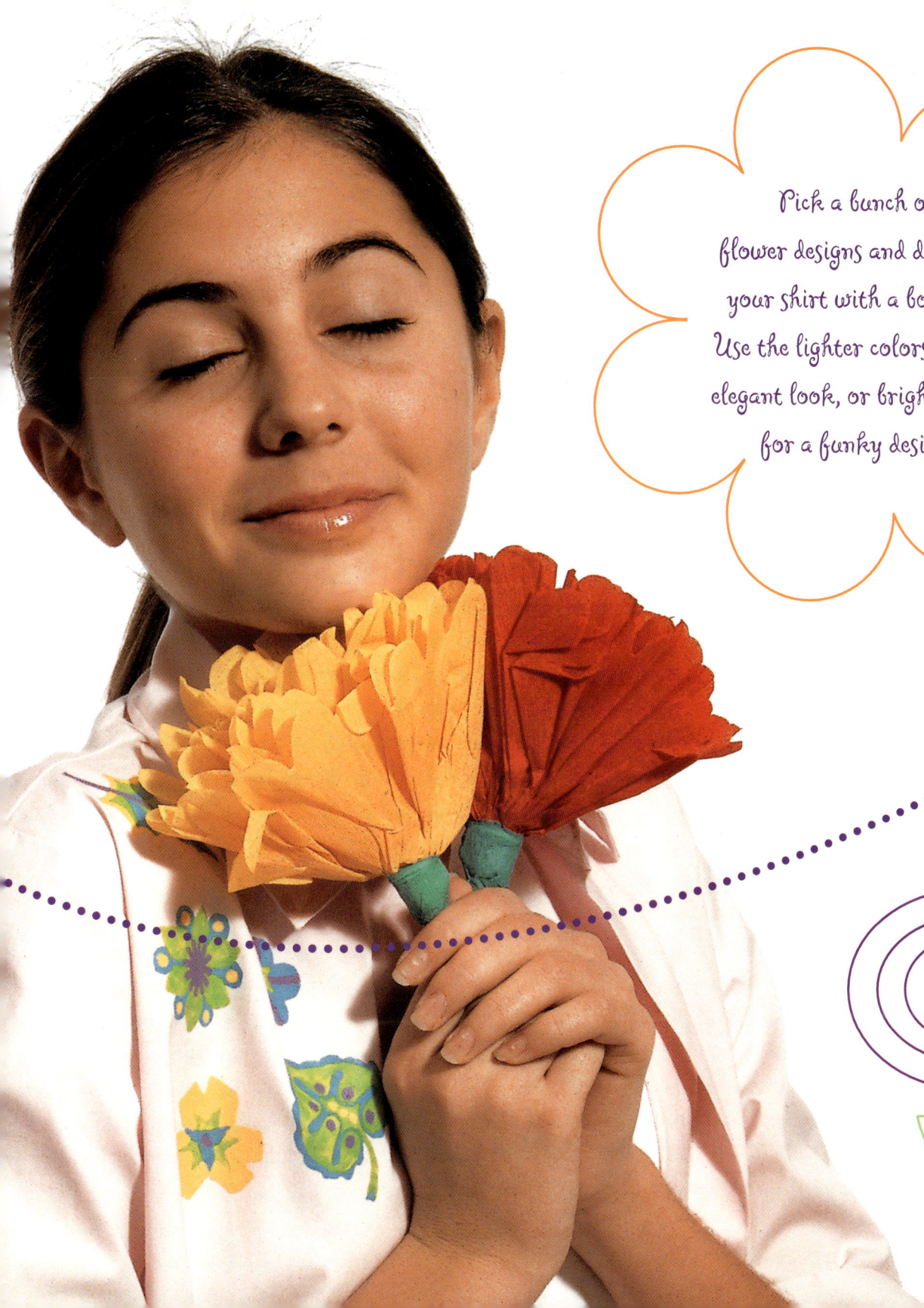

Pick a bunch of flower designs and decorate your shirt with a bouquet. Use the lighter colors for an elegant look, or bright colors for a funky design.

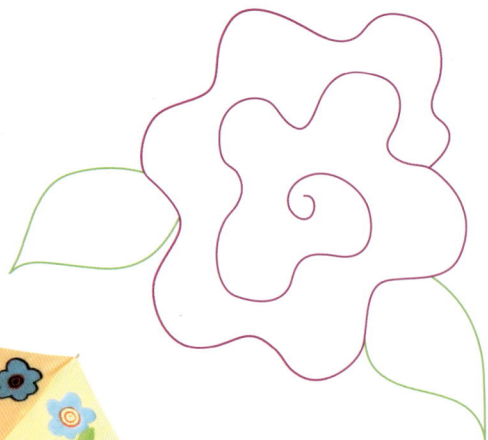

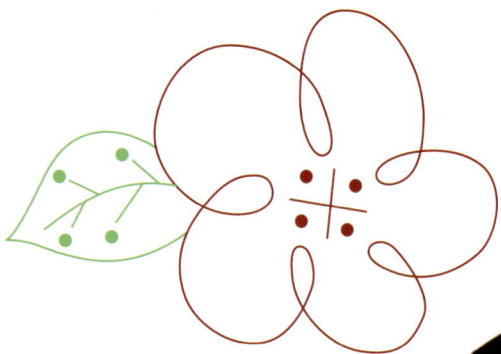

Goodies to Go!

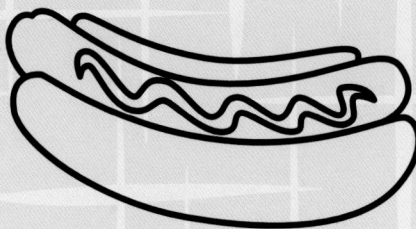

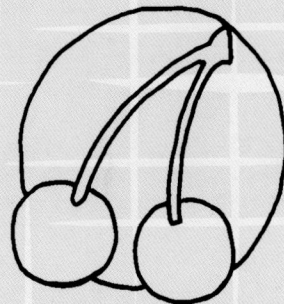

# Beyond the T.

There's more to life than T-shirts! To decorate other fabric things, you may not need an ironing board, but you'll still use an iron and ironing paper. Try out the iron on a test peice of fabric to make sure the temperature won't hurt it. An adult can help you figure out the best way to iron stuff that's not flat.

Fabric-covered journals and albums are simple to decorate— just iron your design directly on the front (don't forget the ironing paper).

To decorate a shoe, put a sock in it. Literally. A balled-up sock stuffed inside the toe of a shoe makes it easier to iron on your design.

Lampshades and umbrellas can be tough. Put a thick oven mitt on your hand to support the fabric under the iron. Work slowly, one transfer at a time.

# Hey, bag lady!

25

# Wild Attire

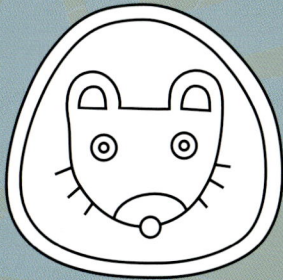
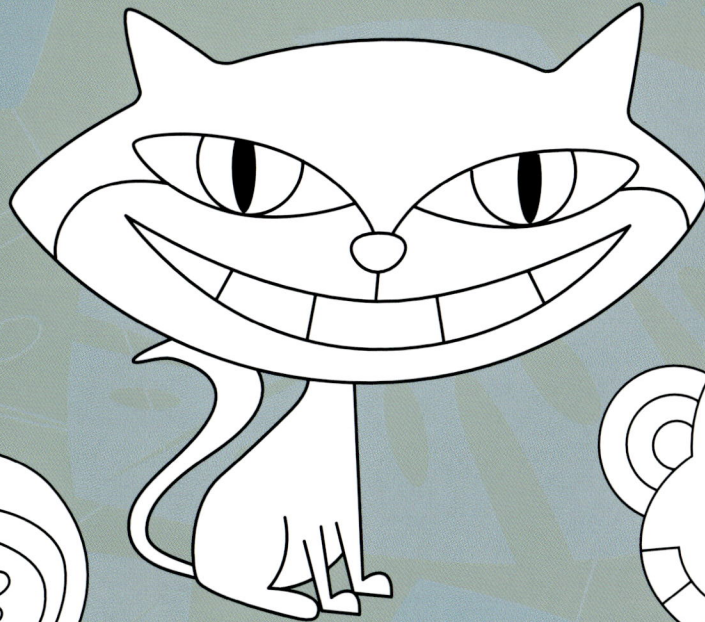

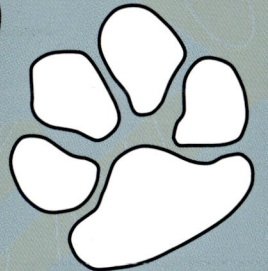

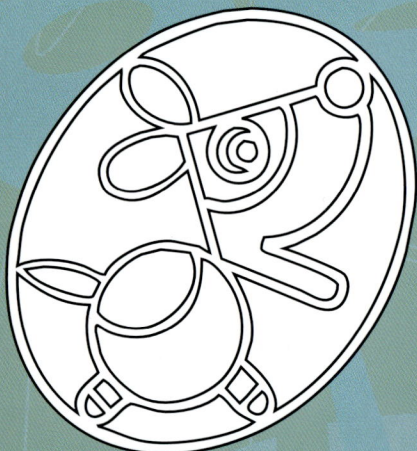

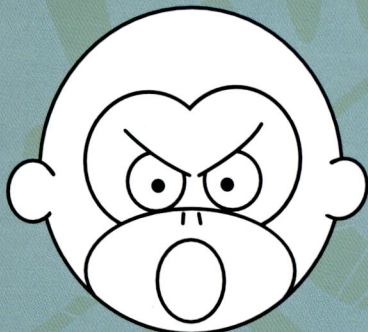

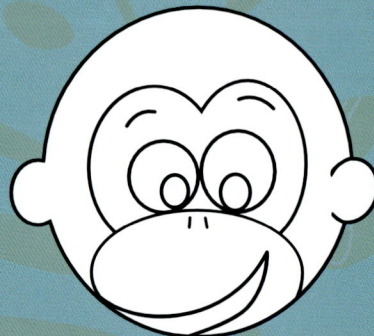

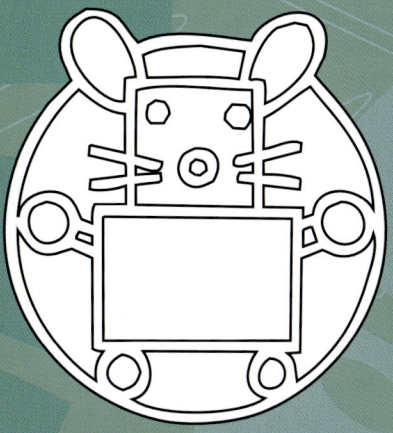
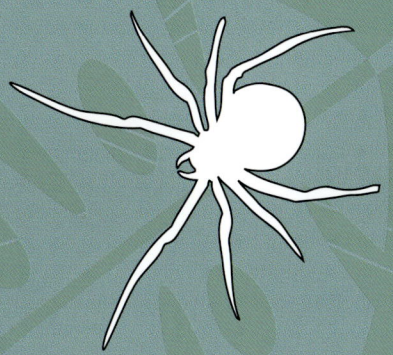

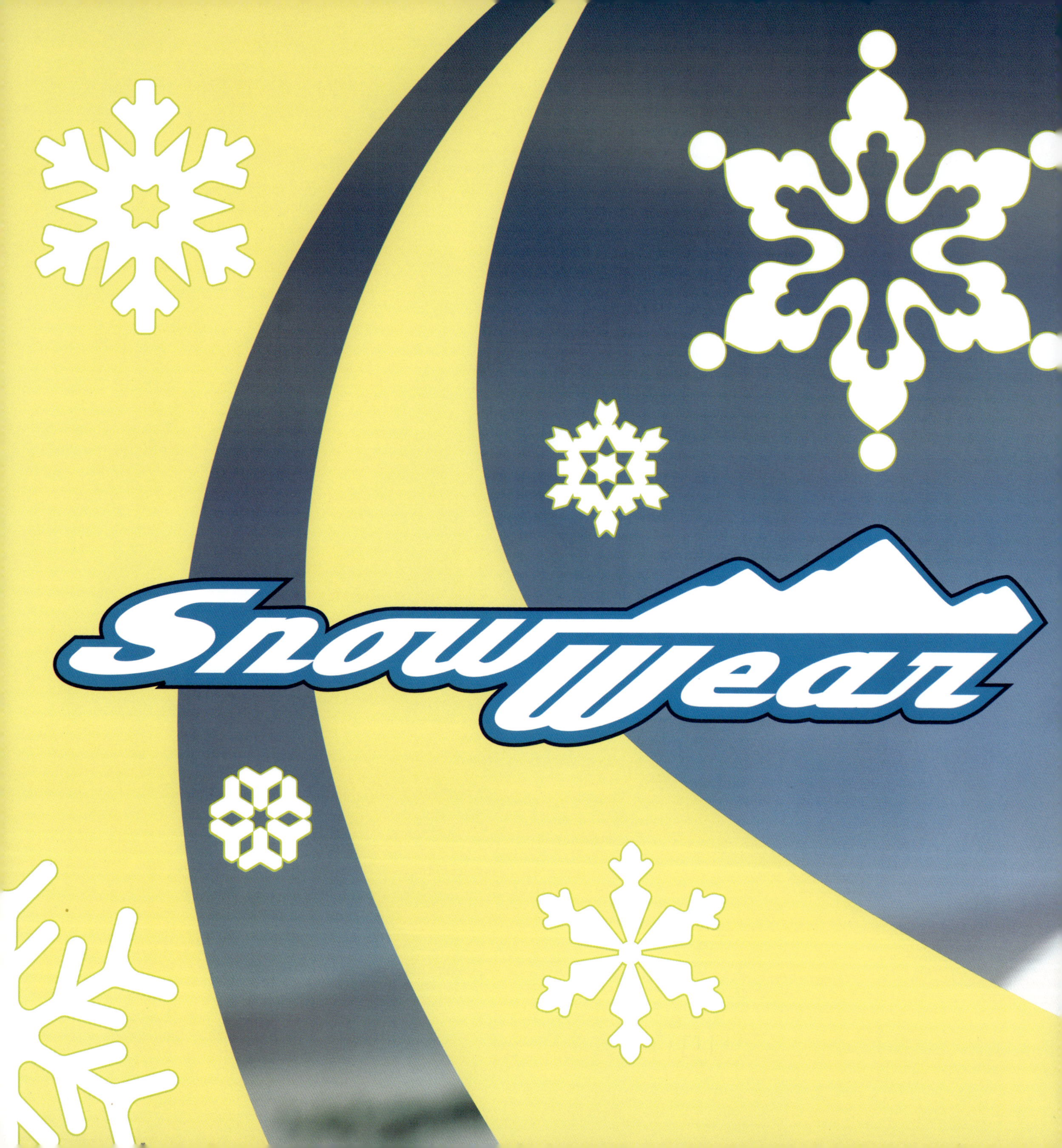
Snow Wear

# StiffyAir

# 900

*Delicate designs like these snowflakes are harder to remove from the plastic.*

# Swiss Cheese

# Nose Grab

# 540

360

BF

720

Misty

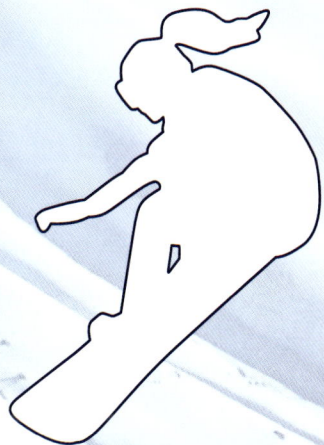

180

cRaZy

24/7

Blah blah, blah

yikes!

yes way

meow

GEEK

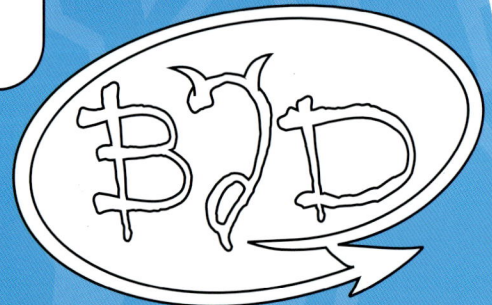

**express** your many **moods** with these **fancy phrases.**

*Change your mood?* **change your shirt!**

**Hi**

Yuk

35

# flĭrt

?

## COMBINE

YOUR initial with a favorite design to make a personalized monogram. OR Spell out YOUR whole name to claim YOUR Stuff.

## Cool
## Babe
## Lucky

A B C D E F

G H I J K L

M N O P Q R

S T U V W X

Y Z

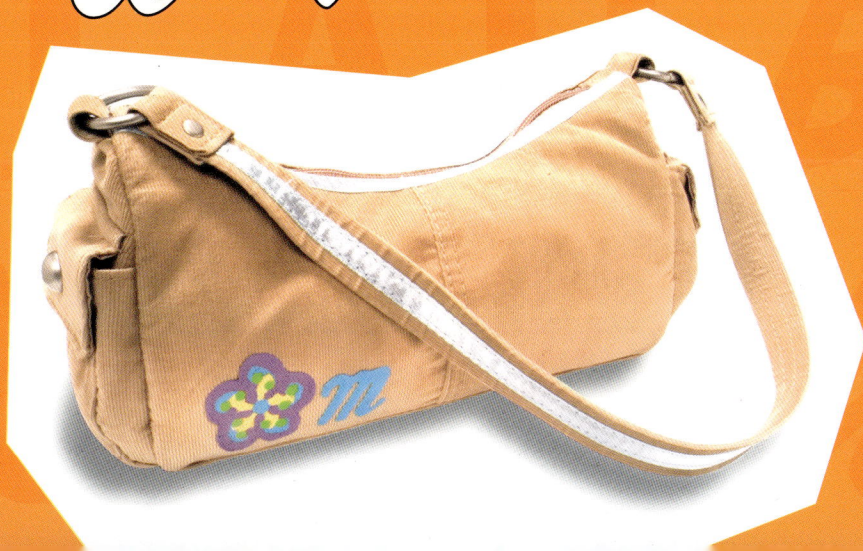

# 1 2 3 4 5
# 6 7 8 9 0

Use a **COMPUTER** to create your own one-of-a-kind phrases. Play around with the font in a word-processing program, print it out, then lay the plastic overlay over the printout. PAINT AS USUAL FOR YOUR OWN *Custom Look!*

Spring Break

2004

duh!

FUN
1

CraZy

Devil

Angel

girl

# love is all you need

**Get that warm and fuzzy feeling by adding a pair of hearts to your slippers.**

**Spread the love to your pajamas, shirt or bag.**

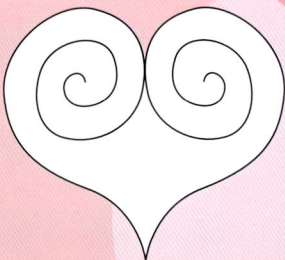

# CULTURE

# couture

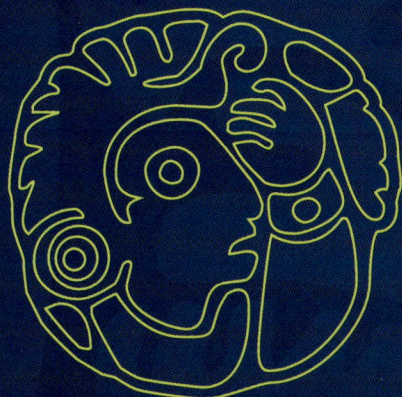

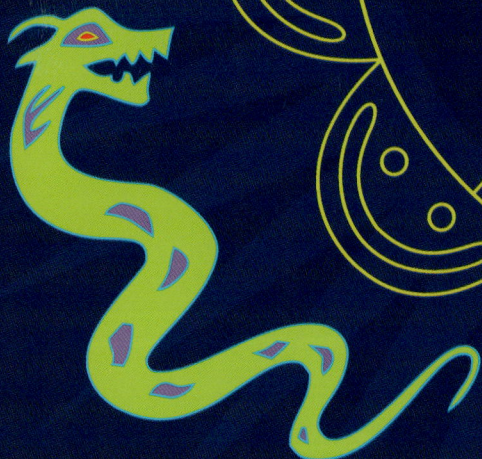

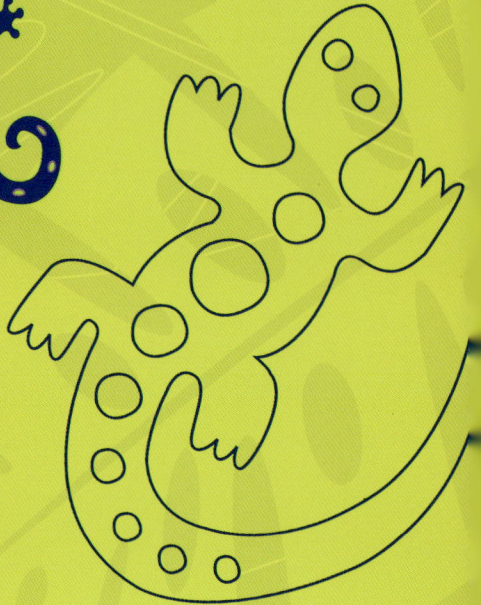

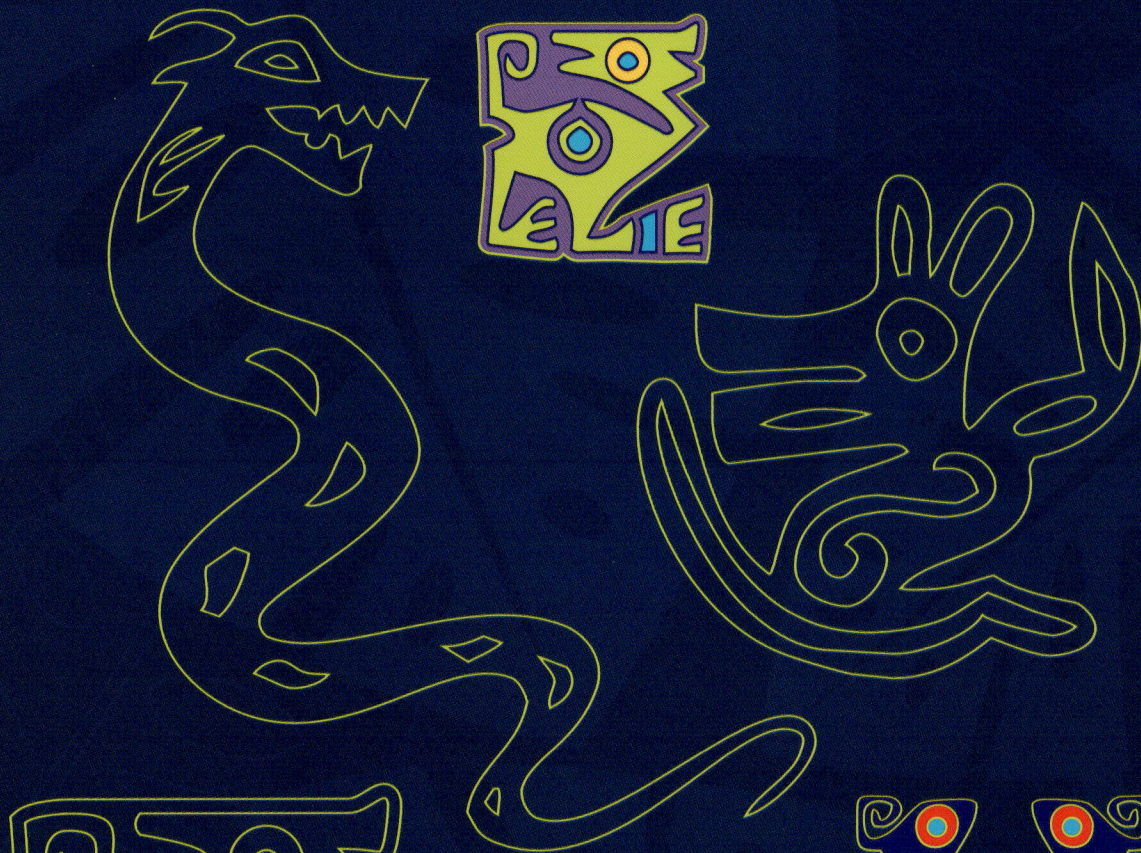

YEEHAW

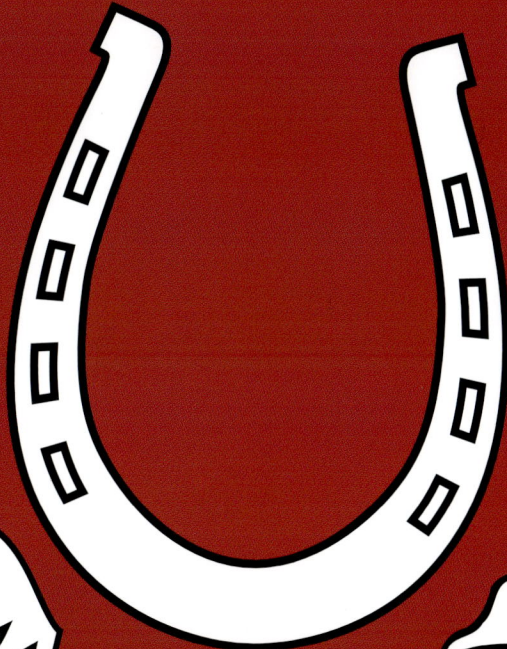

COW  GIRL

# happy
# shirts.

**Super designs of most extreme fashion!**

**Beauty**

**Eternity**

**Heaven**

**Fire**

**Energy**

**Tranquility**

51

Peace. Happiness. And clean T-shirts.

# Sports

# Divas

**Cut & Paste:**
Jina Choi

**Sass Master:**
Megan Smith

**Fashionista:**
Jill Turney

**Development:**
Marilyn Green
Barbara Kane
Eileen Stolee

**Tech Art Diva:**
Sandy Nichols

**Spackle & Photos:**
Matthew Farruggio

**Casting:**
Margaret Farruggio

**Trend Setter:**
Kelly Shaffer

**Crazy Shirtless Man:**
John Cassidy

**Nosy Neighbor:**
Corie Thompson

**Fashion Police:**
Karen Phillips
Gary Mcdonald

**Illustrators:**
Frank Ansley
George Bates
Christine Benjamin
Mague Calanche
Roger Chouinard
John Coulter
Stephan Daigle
Linda Davick
Isabel Dervaux
Jim Dryden
Brian Fujimori
Jack Gallagher
Susan Gross
Jennifer Herbert
Liz Hutnick
Donna Ingemason
Jennifer Kalis
Elizabeth Koebsell
Mary Anne Lloyd
Bill McGuire
Julie Mills
Burton Morris
Joan Parazette
Mary Ross
Steven Salerno
Karen Soleau
Mary Thelen
Erica Thurston
Sandie Turchyn
Martha Vercoutere
Anders Wenngren
Amy Young
Brian Zic

**Models:**
Chelsea Andreatla
Nora Badiner
Stefanie Mateo Benmour
Rachael Chiappetta
Eleni Courcoumelis
Natalie Rae Cressman
Alexandra Goldstein
Ciandra Amaris Keith
Alexandra Lowe
Rebecca Meyer
Mackenzie Nickels
Cathryn Paolini
Alexis Rose
Jana Ross

Juliana Britto Schwartz
Joy Solis-Perry
Sarah Theiner
Jaz Yohai-Rifkin
Lisa the Dog

*Thanks to Barb Magnus and the kids of Stanton Kids Care.*
*Thanks to Eric and Stacey Walstad and Fluffy.*

# DON'T STOP HERE!

USE IMAGES FROM MAGAZINES, BOOKS, POSTCARDS, PHOTOS OR YOUR OWN ART. THE POSSIBLITIES ARE ENDLESS.

• CUT OUT • FILL IN • ADD STAMP • MAIL • WAIT IMPATIENTLY •

CUT OUT • FILL IN • ADD STAMP • MAIL • WAIT IMPATIENTLY •

## Klutz Catalog

You can order more 100% Klutz certified books from the The Klutz Catalog. It is, in all modesty, unlike any other catalog — and it's yours for the asking. Just fill in this postcard, pop on a stamp, drop it in the mail and wait impatiently for your copy to arrive.

## Who are you?

Name: _____ Age: _____ ☐ Too high to count ○ Boy ○ Girl

Address: _____

City: _____ State: _____ Zip: _____

## Tell us more...

What do you think of this book? _____

_____

Comments and compliments here: _____

_____ Complaints here: [  ] Please do not write outside the box.

☐ Check this box if you want us to send you The Klutz Catalog.

If you're a grown-up who'd like to hear about new Klutz stuff, give us your e-mail address and we'll stay in touch.

E-mail address: _____

KLUTZ.com
Come on in!
OPEN 24 HOURS

T-Shirt Art

# Show Us Your Genius!

Send us a photo of your T-Shirt Art creation and it may get displayed on the Fridge of Fame at klutz.com. That's world-wide recognition! To learn more, visit klutz.com or e-mail us at thefridge@klutz.com.

## KLUTZ ®

455 Portage Avenue
Palo Alto, CA 94306

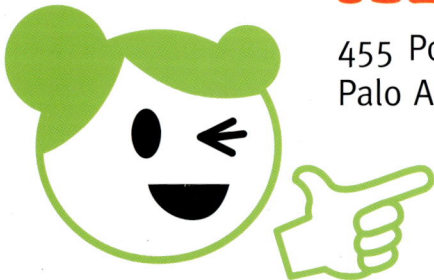